CATS

Louise Van Der Meid

Photo credits: Victor Baldwin, page 11; Carolyn Wohlin, page 31; Walter Chandoha, pages 39 and 42; Arthur Studios, page 44; Kerry Donnelly, page 48; Three Lions, pages 52, 53, 55 and 62. Remaining black and white photos by Louise Van Der Meid.

ISBN 0-87666-173-8

Distributed in the U.S. by T.F.H. Publications, Inc., 211 West Sylvania Avenue, P.O. Box 427, Neptune, N.J. 07753; in England by T.F.H. (Gt. Britain) Ltd., 13 Nutley Lane, Reigate, Surrey; in Canada to the book store and library trade by Clarke, Irwin & Company, Clarwin House, 791 St. Clair Avenue West, Toronto 10, Ontario; in Canada to the pet trade by Rolf C. Hagen Ltd., 3225 Sartelon Street, Montreal 382, Quebec; in Southeast Asia by Y.W. Ong, 9 Lorong 36 Geylang, Singapore 14; in Australia and the South Pacific by Pet Imports Pty. Ltd., P.O. Box 149, Brookvale 2100, N.S.W., Australia; in South Africa by Valiant Publishers (Pty.) Ltd., P.O. Box 78236, Sandton City, 2146, South Africa; Published by T.F.H. Publications, Inc., Ltd., The British Crown Colony of Hong Kong.

CONTENTS

Two kittens are twice the fun, but not twice the bother. Give your kitten a companion and some toys and they are less likely to go looking for trouble.

1. Why Cats Make Good Pets

There are many reasons for selecting kittens as pets. (1) They are so adorable and irresistible, few people can help but want one for a pet. (2) Kittens are inexpensive — sometimes free. (3) They require little care and are less expensive to raise than dogs. (4) Cats are independent and very clean, and adjust to small homes and apartments. (5) Cats are loving companions for lonely elderly people. (6) Cats seem to be elastic where children are concerned. They allow themselves to be lovingly hauled around the house by toddlers and will trustingly purr for more attention. Kittens usually start life with a sympathetic feeling for other babies, whether they are humans, pups, or even birds. Cats will continue to get along with the children and pets in their family, as long as they are not abused or frightened. (7) A kitten can be better therapy for bed patients than toys, books, etc. A sick child will find the antics of a young kitten amusing and time-

Hearing the slightest rustling will send these kittens out on the stalk, whether they are searching out a falling leaf or a passing insect.

Your cat may feel most secure when sleeping next to his owner. It is perfectly safe to let your child sleep with his pet cat, as a matter of fact many children sleep more easily with a cat than with a stuffed toy.

passing when Mother is busy. Cats love an opportunity to nap and purr near an ill adult. This cat companionship keeps many patients from feeling lonely and despondent. Handicapped people and children who cannot leave their homes, often enjoy raising kittens and caring for them. This gives them responsibility and affection from their charges without demanding too much physical stamina. (8) I might add that it really helps to have a cat or two meowing inspiration, if you plan to write a book about them. My cats love to look up at me and "talk" a little, whenever I sit long enough to converse with them. Right now, our Tortoise-shell is trying to tell me all about cat life — if I only had an interpreter!

2. Choosing a Kitten for a Pet

How does one select the kitten best suited for his own family? Your local pet shop can help you. If the pet shop does not have the type of kitten you desire, the manager will have listings of reliable pedigreed cat-breeders and also addresses of new litters of healthy domestic kittens in the neighborhood. Ninety-nine percent of the cats in the U.S.A. are domestic, and the other one percent are the deluxe breeds which include Persians, Siamese, Burmese, Abyssinian, Manx and Blues. A discussion of the *deluxe* breeds of cats will come in another part of this book. Here, we will discuss the safest method of choosing a *domestic* kitten for a pet.

If you have children who are in and out of the house all day and you want a cat that can go in and out with them, the domestic cat is your answer. Pedigreed cats should not be allowed to run loose; because of their value they are apt to be stolen. Then, too, the owner of a pedigreed female cat doesn't want to take a chance of a domestic cat mating with the purebred "queen".

If you are looking for a very reasonable pet for your youngsters or yourself, the pet shops sell healthy, beautiful kittens for approximately $5.00. The long-haired kitten is the prettier provided you have time to brush it daily, otherwise, the short-hair domestic will be better for you as they require practically no grooming.

When the kittens are about 5 weeks old, they will have a full set of baby teeth. It's difficult to tell much about the kittens before this age. At five weeks, you can tell the kittens' personality and health. This is a good time to *put your name* on the one you want, but don't take him from his mother until he is drinking milk, eating cat food and has used a grit box. Domestic kittens should be eight weeks old before taking them away from their mother. The deluxe breed kittens are often three months old before they are sold, so their potential quality can be more readily appreciated.

When selecting the kitten, be certain the eyes are clear and not running. The healthy kitten has a thick glossy coat of fur. Check it for skin infections. A healthy kitten should be active and perky.

It is better to decide (before falling in love with a kitten) the sex you do *not* want; whether you want a male or female and why. If you decide on a young tom, he might make a better pet if neutered before he is a year old. Your veterinarian can advise you when he would prefer to neuter your tom cat and what the expense will be. This operation removes the sperm-producing organs and is a safe and

If you want to keep your cats off the furniture, start training them while they are still kittens. Once the cat has gotten accustomed to resting on the soft cushions of the furniture, it will be a habit hard to break.

minor operation for your male cat, and inexpensive, too. Your neutered male will not become fat if he is not overfed. He will stay at home and seldom get into fights after his operation since he will not have the strong mating urge for which cats are famous.

If you pick a female, she can be spayed by the time she reaches 8 months so that she can never have kittens. This operation for the female is more expensive and also more difficult. It is quite safe, and your cat should be completely recovered from her operation in five days.

Many parents would like their children to have the experience of watching a mother cat and her kittens. Some parents have never had a female cat for their children because they don't know how simple having kittens can be. The mother cat is so capable of taking care of the birth of her kittens and the raising of them, that very little is

8

Tiny enclosures and shiny objects pose Irresistable temptations for curious kittens.

required of her human friends. A cat is such a perfect mother that it is a shame not to let her have at least one or two litters of kittens before she is spayed.

We have two mother cats who have kittens every summer. Our children are still fascinated by the birth of kittens, their mother cats who nurse and wash their kittens, and the development of the sightless kittens until weaned. Our children sympathize with the mother cat when she looks for her babies that have grown up and been given away, they laugh at her when she holds the kittens down for a scrubbing, and they enjoy the responsibility of feeding and caring for the mother cats and their babies. Since city children cannot have the education and fun that comes from raising colts, calves, and farm pets, having kittens is a wonderful substitute. Our children also take an active interest in finding homes for their kittens. They have sold quite a few for 25 cents each and made themselves a dollar spending money on one litter. This enterprise is supervised, of course, and no kittens are sold to their friends without parental approval.

If you have decided you definitely want a female, or if your preference is a male, you can check the sex of the kittens by the time they are eight weeks old. It is easiest to determine the sex of kittens the first week after they are born and then again after 7 or 8 weeks. In the female, the anus and vulva, under the tail, are close together, the one a spot and the other a small slit. In the male, the outlets are two spots and are farther apart than the female's. A three-colored or tortoise-shell cat is almost always a female. Tortoise-shell males are very rare.

The last suggestion I would like to make on choosing a kitten is one seldom mentioned in cat books, but this has been an important factor to me when choosing some dozen kittens for my own family. If you are going to keep your cat in a country home, barn, or store to get rid of mice, choose a barn-cat. His mother has taught him how to catch mice, even if she has neglected his manners a little. If you are an adult with no children, you will get along fine with kittens raised by adults with no children. If you have children and a dog or bird, your kitten will adjust to your family better, if he is already accustomed to children, and dogs or birds. The mother cat who sheaths her claws and purrs contentedly when held by the children in her family will teach her kits to be tame and gentle. Also, the kittens who have been lovingly held and petted by children from the time their eyes were first open, will not be afraid of your children.

My final word on choosing your kitten is: It is really easier to raise two than one. They will keep each company, sleep and play together, and demand less attention from you. If you have more than one youngster, two kittens can share the fondling and not become so exhausted as the little "only kit" who goes from one lap to the next all day long with little time for relaxation. Cats are inexpensive to raise — why not have two?

Three healthy Siamese kittens such as these will pose little problem to the owner who wants to find them loving homes. If you are planning on raising a litter of kittens, be sure that you will be able to place them in homes that will take proper care of them.

This cat may appear to be pondering the passage of time, but he is really trying to devise a way to get at that teasing stream of sand.

3. Care and Training of Kittens

Attempt to bring your kit home in a box or basket, it will feel warm and secure. Remember he has never been in a car before, so if you try to hold him, the strange ride might terrify the kitten.

Be patient and gentle with your new kitten. Keep in mind that it is easier to make him feel at home in one room at a time. Keep your new kitten in a laundry room or bathroom where you can fix a bed for him, then he will get to know you before he can hide under the

This cluster of kittens is shown in momentary repose, for moments such as these are few and far between with healthy, active kittens.

furniture. We have heard of new kittens completely disappearing in their new homes, only to come strolling out from under some over-stuffed chair three days after their owners had thought them lost forever. Forewarned is forearmed! Keep him in a room where he cannnot hide under a bed or inside a TV set until he has had several meals from you and is no longer frightened by his new surroundings.

A kitten loves any kind of a box or basket for a bed. Old towels no longer pretty on the towel rack, make warm soft liners for the kittens' bed and can be laundered often. Very attractive cat-basket beds and pillows are for sale in the pet stores. The cat will like either box or basket, but the basket is, of course, more attractive if your cat plans to sleep in a part of the house that you keep pretty.

Before tucking your kitten in his bed for the first night, give him a little bedtime snack. Evaporated milk and warm water on a saucer and a little of the same brand of cat-food *that he has been eating* will help keep him from waking up hungry in the *middle* of the night.

After he has eaten, put him in the flat pan or box of deodorized grit that you have fixed for him. Keep putting him in, until he "squats." Now, he is ready to be put in bed. If he cries, you may find putting a stuffed toy (or small hot water bottle wrapped in a towel) in his box will give him something to snuggle to. These first few nights away from his mother are easier on you if you selected two kittens. They keep each other company and do not feel as lonely as the *only-child* does.

You should feed your new kitten at least four times daily at first. His diet can consist of evaporated milk and warm water, cat food, a little garlic chopped in food to prevent worms and gradually bits of meat from the table.

If you do not want a cat odor in your house, do *not* train your cat to a box of dirt or sand. Buy a bag of *deodorized* grit from your pet-shop. One bag will usually last until the kitten can go outdoors, unless you live in a cold climate. First, put down a newspaper and then a flat pan with a couple handfuls of grit. This grit absorbs the odors and can be changed whenever it gets wet. Large catteries have grit racks and dry the used grit in the sun. This way is the economical way and the grit trays can be used over again, saving the cost of daily changing. One or two little kittens won't use very much grit, and their's should be changed daily if you are as fussy about keeping them odorless as I am. You continue to place the kitten in the grit after each meal, until the gets the idea. Do not let him run the

Dangling ornaments such as these just invite the play of kittens, who can't resist taking a swat at most anything that moves. Training your cat as to where they can and cannot play should alleviate all temptations.

A well trained cat will let you know when he wants to go outside without scratching on the door. This cat sits peacefully on his favorite piece of carpet for his owner to let him out.

Opposite: If you choose to let your kitten play outside, be sure to buy him a collar with his name on it and a flea collar for protection against parasites.

house unsupervised, until he is trained. If you do catch him starting to use another spot — scold him and put him in his grit. When cleaning the grit pan, use hot water and soap. Do not use strong disinfectants, as these will make your kitten sick and he'll never use his grit pan again.

As soon as your kitten is adjusted to your house, you can start taking him outdoors. He will have a heavier coat and better appetite if not kept in the house constantly. If you have a fenced in yard protected from stray dogs, he can play out in mild weather unsupervised. Do not leave him alone outdoors where he can get into the street, follow a youngster and get lost, or be attacked by a dog, until he is old enough to get up a tree and take care of himself.

Some cats prefer to sleep in the house in the daytime and prowl outdoors at night. This may really be safer, as there is less traffic at night. Our Kansas cats loved to sleep up a shady tree during the daytime as the house was too hot for them in California. They were protected from dogs, and they never fell out of a tree when asleep. We humans have to sometimes adjust to our cats' habits. It has been often said "we don't own a cat, they own us".

As your kitten gets older, it is a good idea to train him to use a scratching-post instead of clawing your furniture. Pet-shops sell scratching posts, or they can be made by tacking carpet around a post with a heavy base that won't topple over. A little catnip around the post will encourage your kittens to use scratching-post instead of furniture. A folded newspaper can be used to scold a growing cat from clawing furniture; the sound alone will do the trick. If your cat refuses to cooperate it will be safer for your best sofa or chair if you keep him out of the living-room until he can behave and not sharpen his claws on your best furnishings.

It is a good idea to have your kitten checked by a veterinarian. The vet can check your kitten for ringworm with a special lamp and he can also give the kitten any necessary distemper and rabies shots.

Ask your vet for a safe flea powder if you need it. Don't use dog medicines on cats. Do not use strong laxatives on cats. A little sardine oil once a week will help keep your cat free of fur balls.

When your kitten or cat acts sick or listless, you can take his temperature rectally and then call the veterinarian. You should not try to doctor a sick cat without a vet's help. Even trimming a cat's claws is a delicate job and should be left to a vet or pet-shop groomer.

4. Children and Kittens

This may be the first time in your youngster's lifetime that you've had the opportunity to teach him gentleness and responsibility toward a new pet. The earlier these rules are learned, the happier both children and pets will be together.

Our children have *always* had cats, so they grew up knowing how

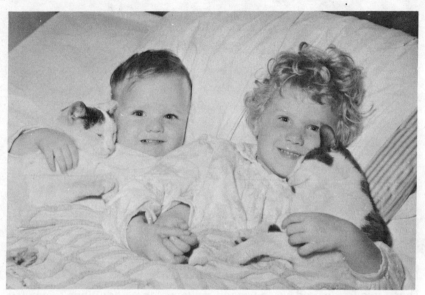

Cats are natural playmates for children, provided that the play does not get too rough for the cat's well being.

pets should be treated. Our first cat "Olee" was given to us by a neighbor because as a half-grown kitten "Olee" adopted our baby, Lynne, and entertained her by the hour in her playpen. "Olee" travelled from California to New York State with us. He was content to eat left-over formula and baby food and "baby-sit" for us while we drove.

By the time Rob was 2 years old, he took *his* cat to bed with him instead of a stuffed toy. As soon as Rob was contentedly lulled to sleep by his cat's purring lullaby, we quietly removed "Tigerlily" for the night. Cats are clean companions for youngsters, but not good bedfellows, as they usually decide to play with the blankets or scamper around the room in the middle of the night. The idea of a cat delib-

These two longhaired kittens would make welcome additions to any loving home, but since they are still small and somewhat frail they should not be handled by very young children.

erately trying to suffocate a baby seems more of a *wives' tale* than truth; however, common sense would keep mothers on guard to keep cats out of small babies' cribs when the babies are asleep and alone, if only for sanitary reasons.

Since our children have always wanted and loved their cats, they enjoy taking care of them now. Caring for a kitten is a wonderful education in responsibility for any youngster. A parent might have to remind youngsters if they sometimes forget to feed their kittens but the daily feeding chores soon become a habit.

If your children have never had a pet, they may be rough with their first kitten. Be firm, but patient, while the adjustment to a new pet is being made. Cruel abuse of a pet should be punished at the time it happens. It is up to the parent to set the rules and enforce them. A new kitten is still a baby and should not be handled more than a few minutes at a time. He still needs lots of sleep.

If your toddler has a new baby sister or brother this is a good time for him to own a pet. A kitten will be a loving companion while his mom is spending time with a new baby.

A parent can teach his youngster gentleness by gently patting the new kitten with the child's hand, and removing the kitten to another room, if the child gets loud or rough.

Many adult cats have the best of both worlds: being able to roam and exercise outside when they like, returning to their family for food, affection and shelter.

If your young toddler shows no signs of gentleness after a few weeks of scoldings, or if he is an extremely active noisy young fellow of whom your kitten is afraid maybe you had better find another home for this kitten, until your guy is older and more settled down. Even gentle kittens will grow mean and bite and scratch if they are dropped, kicked, pulled by the tail, or squeezed with vengeance. Yet, I have seen full-grown purring cats lovingly carried by small youngsters who could only get the middle of the cat off the floor, both front and back

Assigning children the task of feeding their cats daily will teach them to be responsible pet owners and will build a bond of affection between owner and pet.

ends of the happy cat could be dragging, and as long as the child talked lovingly to his cat, the cat uncomfortably, but contentedly submitted.

It is up to the parents to teach their youngsters that this new kitten is not just another toy that can be kicked around. Your youngster can help you feed and brush the cat and at the same time he should be taught not to experiment on the cat by cutting off his whiskers or poking at him roughly. If we show our youngsters how to gently love and handle kittens, they usually cooperate in a short time.

5. Kittens and Other Pets

If you already have a cat he may not accept a new kitten in his home without putting up a fuss. Do not leave a new kitten alone with your cat until they are well acquainted and friendly. If your cat persists in slapping the newcomer it would be a good idea to have your pet-shop groomer trim the big cat's claws. Usually cats will get along with a new kitten after a few days. If the older cat persists in acting jealous and mean to the kitten after a week or more, it would be wiser not to force the situation. Find another home for one of them.

Cats and dogs can be the best of friends as long as they are socialized from an early age to accept each other. Pet owners should make it a point to show an equal amount of attention to each of their pets to avoid any possible jealousies.

Two kittens of about the same age will get along beautifully. When your mother cat has kittens, she will get along with one of her own litter, if you decide to keep one kitten. Any other combination will have to be tried out with supervision.

Many people think that dogs and cats do not get along together. We have *always* had a dog with our kittens. Our first dog was a Springer Spaniel, and our cat's favorite "kitten sitter." She completely entrusted her wee little babies to our pup. When the cat was killed by an explosion, our Springer sadly looked for his cat friend for many months.

These pals don't subscribe to the belief that they should be "fighting like cats and dogs."

Our cutest trio was our two mother cats, Bootsie and Budgie, and a parti-color Cocker named Parti-boy. These three played, ate, and slept together. The Cocker was lonesome and whined if we did not put a cat in the laundry-room with him every night.

If you have a dog and want to add a kitten to your household, give them a few days under the same roof with supervision and they will probably become good companions.

Our present upstart of a Silver-Buff Cocker pup thinks he is the

The domesticated cat of today still retains their stalking instinct, yet this in no way interferes with their being loving, affectionate housepets.

new boss at our house. Bootsie and Budgie accept him and even trust him with their kittens. In order that the cats get their share at dinner time, we find it best to feed them in private so that our hungry pup doesn't gobble their dinner, too.

Many a "cat chasing" dog will accept a new kitten in his own home and still chase the neighbor's cats away at every chance. Do not leave a new kitten alone with a dog until you can trust them together. Be sure you do not make such a big fuss over the new kitten that the old dog feels jealous. Give the dog more attention than ever, and he will be more apt to make friends with your new kitten.

A full grown cat is a little more difficult to handle with a rambunctious puppy. First, you had better have the vet trim her claws. Give your cat lots of loving and affection and don't concentrate entirely on the new pup. Don't leave your pup with a cat unprotected, until he is big enough to hold his own. Here again, a cat and pup will soon realize they must get along together in the same household. Some pair off and become affectionate "buddies", other cat and dog combinations just accept each other. They aren't exactly pals, but they don't fight either.

It is a cat's natural instinct to hunt birds, and yet many homes have both cats and birds for pets. Your pet shops are good examples of how a trusted cat can be allowed to roam cage after cage of birds. One Siamese cat I know makes no attempt to bother the many birds that even fly loose around him in a pet-shop.

I do not recommend that a new cat should be left alone with your bird, but with proper precautions they can live together under the same roof. A new kitten will adapt itself to the pets in his own household. It is not wise to allow your bird out of his cage when the kitten is in the house. Keep your bird-cage high, hung from a hook would be the safest, if you own a kitten or cat. Spank your cat with a rolled newspaper if he ever goes after your bird. Never leave your cat and bird alone together. Put them in separate rooms when you leave the house.

Kittens will also learn to get along with other pets such as bunnies, ducklings, cavies, etc. These pets need supervision until they become acquainted and are good friends.

6. Why Not Have Kittens?

Your female cat will be mature after eight months and will come in season by the time she is one year old. If you have children, they will learn more biological facts from watching their cat have kittens than most parents could possibly explain to them. A child who has watched the birth of any pet will not be afraid to discuss those natural questions with his parents in a wholesome natural manner. The cat is "matter-of-fact" about her pregnancy, birth of her kittens, and post-natal care. Adults can learn a lot watching their *purring* mother-cat deliver her babies. No fear, no complaints. She is just proud of her new babies and full of happiness. Why not enjoy some kittens in your home? The mother cat will take complete charge of the birth and care of her kittens with very little help from you.

First, I think it's a shame to let a half-grown kitten be rushed into motherhood too early. She is apt not to care for her kittens as well as a mature cat. If your kitten comes in season at six or seven months, try to keep her in the house until she is eight or nine months old and better prepared to raise a family.

You can tell when your cat is in season because she gets unusually coy and playful. Even our 6-year old grandmother cat acts kiddish and

This female Siamese is receiving plenty of nourishment during her pregnancy, which should aid her in producing a healthy litter of kittens.

If you have two cats of different sexes, it is best to have at least one of them neutered to avoid having unwanted litters of kittens. Females are generally spayed when between six and eight months old, which is when they are nearly full grown and mature. Males can be neutered any time after six months of age, and this relatively simple operation will make for a better pet as it limits his desire to roam.

Opposite: If you notice that your unspayed female is coming into heat and you do not want her to have a litter, be sure to keep her inside and away from all unaltered males.

flirtatious every Spring. You may notice a slight discharge at this time. Your pet shop or vet will check for you, if you are in doubt. When the neighborhood toms come "a-courting", you can be sure your female cat invited them. If the neighbors are unhappy, because of the

This little girl stayed up most of the night to watch over her pet while she had kittens to be sure that nothing went wrong.

tom-cat serenades at mid-night, you can pacify them by keeping your female cat in the house nights while she is in heat.

Once your cat is pregnant, she will settle down again. Our cats even have morning sickness for a few days. At this time your cat should be fed plenty of calcium, minerals, and vitamins. If your cat doesn't care for milk, ask your pet shop for a good calcium powder that can be stirred into food. Raw eggs will help to keep your cat's fur glossy.

Many a kitten with good intentions has found himself up a tree without a ladder!

If you have any prize begonias, be sure to keep them out of reach of your cats as they love to munch on those tasty greens. If your cat is to be a strictly indoor cat, try to provide them with some kitty grass (available at your pet shops) which will fulfill their desires for chlorophyll.

A cat's pregnancy lasts nine weeks or less. When your cat's tummy begins to fill out, and she looks into your drawers and closets for a nest, her time is getting near. Both of our cats, Bootsie and Budgie, tag me around the house the day before their kittens arrive. We pick out a quiet isolated room or closet for them. They prefer a large flat box to have their kittens in. They brace their legs against the sides of the box when their labor pains begin.

I fix the box with clean but old material or towel for a lining. Some people shred newspapers in their box. Every night for a week before the kittens are due, I tuck the expectant mother in her box. She may

This mother cat is bringing her wandering child back to the flock! A good mother becomes nervous if she cannot readily see all her kittens at once.

not act interested in the maternity box, but when I open the door in the morning, she is always asleep in it.

Bootsie and Budgie both like me to be around when their kittens are coming. I try to stay with them as much as I can after their contractions start. Sometimes, Lynne, Rob, and I quietly take turns staying with our cats until all of their kittens are born. We talk softly to our cats, offer them milk and pet them. We never allow strangers or a *gang* of youngsters in our cat maternity room, as the expectant cat might decide to have her kittens behind the TV-set or some such spot if she is frightened by noise or strange people around at this time.

Our cats usually let out one loud cry of warning, before their labor pains get strong. I take them to their box and get them a saucer of milk. They start purring and waiting. If they don't object, I leave them for awhile and check off and on to see that everything is alright, until they start to pant and get restless.

The first time my little girl watched her cat have kittens, she said, "I just want to watch Budgie *lay* one more." She did look like she was a hen laying eggs, as she discreetly sat with her back to us, while each kitten was born.

Each kitten arrives encased in a membrane sac. The kitten either breaks the sac as it is born, or the mother cat opens it with her teeth. She also severs the umbilical cord, eats the sac, cleans up the kittens and starts them nursing. The hormones in the sac help prepare the mother cat for her nursing duties.

Young kittens must be handled very gently and carefully. This youngster is getting a lesson on how to properly pick up and hold a kitten.

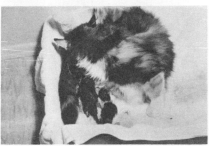

A tortoiseshell longhair gives birth to a litter of kittens: Top picture shows her during labor. In the second photo she attends the latest arrival as it begins to present itself. In the third she is licking and cleaning the newborn. The fourth and bottom photos show the mother cat settling down into her box to allow the newest kitten and his littermates to nurse.

The normal birth of an average litter of four kittens takes about two hours. If your cat's labor-pains run over twelve hours, and she is not able to deliver her kittens normally, take her to your nearest veterinarian.

We have had close to thirty litters of kittens with only one slight mishap. Our mother cat became excited delivering her first litter, and accidentally bit off one kitten's tail when biting the cord. The little kitten didn't suffer, and grew to be a darling bobtail cat.

After the kittens are all born, the mother is exhausted. We praise her and tell her how pretty her kittens are, and she contentedly goes to sleep purring and nursing her new brood.

Usually the mother cat stays in her box for 12 to 24 hours after her busy delivery. When she goes outdoors to relieve herself for the first time, I change the soiled lining in the kitten box. It is a good idea to check the sex of the kittens while changing the box as the least amount of handling the better until the kitten's eyes are open.

The kittens are born blind, deaf, toothless and helpless. Except for their small round tiger-like ears, kittens resemble mice when first born. The kittens are soon able to smell, taste and hear. In fact, I

Siamese kittens such as these are among the most popular of the cat breeds. It should be very easy to place these kittens in loving homes.

36

have seen kittens not more than two days old spit at our snoopy dog, when he looked in at them.

Our children never handle their kittens, until the babies' eyes are wide open. This gives the kits from eight days to two weeks without handling. At first, the kittens' eyes are very sensitive to bright light, and they should be kept in a dimly lit room. Except for my changing the lining in their box each day, the mother cat takes complete care of her charges for the first month. At a month, the first set of baby teeth begin to grow in. This set of teeth begins to come out when the kitten is five months old.

When the kittens are more than a month old, they will start to lap up evaporated milk and warm water from a saucer. The mother cat will show her children how to lap up milk though sometimes it is necessary to gently push their faces into the milk. The kittens will rapidly learn to drink milk and eat cat food.

Once the kittens begin to climb in and out of their box, you can take them outdoors on warm days for a few minutes at a time to relieve themselves. You should fix a grit pan for the house.

Between the time the kittens are six and eight weeks old, your children should enjoy them the most. Kittens are so cute and full of mischief at this age. Unfortunately, now it is time to find a good home for the kits. Usually the pet shop where you buy your pet supplies will help you. It is often helpful to leave your name and address with your veterinarian, too. Quite often people who have just lost a cat will ask their vet if he knows where they can find a kitten. We tell the postman, milkman, teachers at school and all of our friends when we have kittens available and always have more calls than cats. Our minister once announced in an evening meeting that "the Van der Meid's were looking for homes for three Methodist kittens." Finding homes for your kittens takes a little advertising, but the fun and education your children get from the experience is well worth the effort.

Tight squeezes are often the favorite spots for mischevious kittens.

Opposite: Won't the owner of this top hat be surprised to find he has just supplied this comfort-seeking cat with a luxurious bed of his own.

7. Historical Background

There are fewer breeds of tame cats than dogs. Man appreciates a dog's loyalty and obedience. A cat, on the other hand, is self-sufficient and nobody's servant. She teaches herself to hunt for mice and comes to her master only when it suits her. She is clean, affectionate, and beautiful, which are reasons for her survival as a family pet since before Christianity.

A cat became a cat about forty million years ago. They developed from the civet side of the cat family and are distant cousins to the saber-toothed tiger. The first cats in Egypt probably descended from African wildcats. The Egyptians were known to tame cats as early as 3000 B.C. and cats were owned by the wealthy Egyptians. During this period in feline history, cats were adored and even embalmed with their masters at death. The Abyssinian breed descended from early Egyptian cats. Tame cats from Egypt were imported into Italy by Phoenician traders before Christianity. Cats were also known in Greece and Rome before the Christian era.

In Europe, Egyptian cats mated with European wildcats. By the 5th century A.D., cats were in China, Netherlands, and Scotland. Early Christians associated cats with witches and the devil was often depicted in the form of a black cat. This was a black period in cat history, and cats were brutally tortured and killed by superstitious and frightened mobs. Millers and sailors stayed loyal to their cat companions and mousers in spite of superstitions that caused most cats to be destroyed throughout Europe in the 15th Century.

The earliest record of cats in Great Britain dates from 936 A.D. when Howel Oda, prince of South Central Wales, enacted a law for their protection. The cat came to America with the colonists. During the gold rush in 1849, mice and rats threatened the health and food supplies of miners. When the S.S. Ohio docked in San Francisco the miners paid as high as $50.00 for a single cat. Today more than 27,000,000 cats in the U.S.A. help fight one-half billion rodents.

Speaking of cats as mousers, here are some facts that show why they are such excellent natural hunters. All cats are carnivores. The cat's tongue is rough which helps him lap up food and also helps him wash himself. Cats must have no odor to frighten away mice, so they keep themselves spotlessly clean. A cat can make leaps 7 feet in the air, and his long tail helps balance him. All cats except Cheetahs

Today's domesticated cat exhibits the fine lines, grace and allure that have been the cat's trademark through time. This adult is a fine example of the tabby markings that are found on many felines.

have retractable claws. A cat has 18 claws, 5 on each forefoot and 4 on each hind foot. A cat cannot see in absolute darkness, but it needs much less light than any other common animal. Their convex eyes collect

This expressive kitten is making his displeasure about posing next to the halloween jack-o-lantern perfectly clear!

light from a wide angle. The cats long whiskers are useful to him for hunting in the dark. His whiskers are sensitive and warn him of danger. Our pet housecats to-day inherit all of these physical aids for hunting, plus cunning and courage, from such wildcats as the Puma, Lynx, Tiger, Cheetah, Ocelot, and Bobcat.

What more could the well cared for cat ask for than a set-up such as this? This ingenious owner has devised a system where his cats can come and go as they please, and has constructed his entrances and exits with a stylish flair.

Well-bred Siamese cats, such as this sleek adult, comprise less than 1% of the number of cats in this country. Domestic shorthairs outnumber their purebred relatives 99 to 1.

Children are always asking questions such as "How does a cat purr?" Compton's *Encyclopedia* gives an excellent answer to this question. "In the cat's voice box or larynx, there are two sets of vocal cords. The lower are the true cords. The cat uses them to produce meowing and howling sounds. Above these are prominent membranes called false cords. When a cat is happy, it relaxes the lower cords, so that they make no sound and lets the air play against the upper membranes. Some wildcats such as the Tiger, Lynx, and Puma also purr."

Commercial catteries such as this one are owned by breeders who deal in large numbers of litters per year. Each cage is spacious enough to house two or three cats until they are sold to good homes.

In 1953 a cat-food company discovered in a survey that there were twice as many farm cats as city cats. It also indicated 29% of the nation's families had one or more cats, and that low income families had more cats than high income families. In this nation, 99% of the cats are classified as domestic short-hairs, and 1% includes all of the deluxe breeds which are: Persian, Siamese, Burmese, Abyssinian, Manx, and Russian Blue. The leading cat organizations in the U.S. include: American Cat Association, The Cat Fanciers' Federation, and The United Cat Federation. In most cat shows there are four classes:

1. Kittens — 4-8 months old.
2. Novice — for cats which have not won a 1st prize.
3. Open — for all cats that have not won championships.
4. Championship — for all cats who have won 1st prizes in the Novice, Open, or Championship classes.

Conscientious breeders have worked for many generations to improve the quality of the litters produced in their breed. This fine Siamese cat illustrates the sleek lines and distinctive points that are characteristic of the breed. Those who are interested in producing the best quality possible—whether they breed Pekingese pups or Siamese kittens—stress that fine specimens come from well-planned breeding programs, not from haphazard matings.

8. Deluxe Breeds of Cats

BURMESE

The Burmese cat was originally a color variety of the Siamese. The Burmese originated in Burma. This breed was imported into the U.S.A., from India, in 1930. The original Burmese was lighter brown in color than is now being raised for show. The Burmese originally had points, but now its coat is solid dark brown without points. The eyes are golden rather than blue. It is docile and friendly, even more affectionate than the Siamese. The Burmese has a voice similar to the Siamese.

MANX

The first Manx landed in 1588 and were picked up by the Spanish. The ancestors of the Manx cat came from the Isle of Man. The Manx has no tail. Its short back and high legs give it a hoppy gait. The Manx is energetic but very shy with strangers. He is lovable and intelligent. He is not only a good mouser, but he will hunt snakes too. The Manx has a double coat which makes him more comfortable in an outdoor pen than in a warm house. The Manx has a short coat of fur in blue grey, tabby patterns, etc. He has a very quiet voice and makes a loving companion and pet.

ABYSSINIANS

The Abyssinian breed of cat came from Abyssinia or Ethiopia. This cat is a close relative of the ancient sacred Egyptian cat. After World War I there were approximately 25 Abyssinian cats in England. This cat was introduced into the U.S. about 1936. Its ticked coat resembles that of a Belgian hare. This breed has a reddish brown coat with markings of black, grey, or brown. It must have no white spots. The good Abyssinian has black at end of his tail, black between the toes, black hocks, but should not have a black spineline. There should be three ticks on each hair, giving the cat the appearance of its hair standing up instead of smooth.

The Abyssinian has a beautiful bell-like meow. They are similar to a Siamese in sweet disposition without the noisy voice of the Siamese to express their affection. The Abyssinian cat looks more like a miniature wild-cat than the other breeds. It is beautiful, very clean, and still quite rare. The kittens for pets (not show which cost more) cost $75.00 and up.

Be sure to supply your cat with a scratching post to sharpen his claws on, or you may find your furniture tattered before its time.

These valuable cats and kittens require even more careful grooming and feeding than the Persian and Siamese. They are never allowed to run free without supervision. When my children are old enough to keep the doors closed and not let a valuable cat run loose, I should love to have one of these feline aristocrats. My heart was captured by a darling Abyssinian kitten named Junior, while taking the cat pictures for this book. If he has a grandson around in a few more years, he would be my choice for a pet.

The Russian Blue cat is seen more in England than in the U.S.A. This breed is called Foreign Blue in England. It was first imported from Archangel, Russia to Denmark and then England. This breed is still very rare in the U.S.

The Russian Blue has a thick double coat of fur like a seal. The fur is bright blue, almost lavender. Their skin is blue too. The eyes are green. They have shorter and rounder tails than the Siamese. They are affectionate and very quiet. These kittens are quite expensive, as the Russian Blue Mother cat usually only has one or two in each litter. She should not be bred more than once a year.

The care and grooming facts found in the chapter on Siamese cats would also apply to the DeLuxe breeds in this chapter.

9. Persian Cats

The long-haired Persian cat may be derived from the Pallos wildcat of Asia. The Angora long-haired cat originally was from Angora, Turkey. The Angora has been interbred with Persians until it is no longer a separate breed. Persian cats and kittens are majestic and beautiful. Most Persian kittens like affection and get along with children, especially if they start their lives in a home with children. One must expect a long-haired cat to be reserved and quiet, even so the Persians are hardy and can adjust to indoor or outdoor living.

Persian kittens should not leave their mothers until they are nine to fourteen weeks old. A healthy and strong Persian kitten can be purchased for $25.00 and up. Persians come in a large variety of colors. The tortoise-shell is black, red, and yellow and is almost always a female. Solid colors should be pure and can be white, black, orange, cream, or blue. The silver or chinchilla Persian has a snow white coat, and each hair is tipped with black. The Persian tabby should have a light ground color with contrasting stripes, spots, or bars.

A blue-eyed white Persian should be checked for deafness. This particular combination can inherit a tendency toward deafness. Some blue-eyed white Persians are partially deaf, and some are totally deaf. It is not uncommon for a white Persian to have one green eye and one blue eye. The fact that the Persian's eyes are different colors does not affect their sight, nor their value.

The care of your Persian kitten is much the same as that of the domestic kitten, except for more grooming and less freedom for her. In addition to the supply of cat food, deodorizing grit, scratching-post, and basket or box-bed from your pet shop, you will want to select a good cat brush and comb for your Persian. Your long-haired cat should be combed and brushed every day. Don't comb the fur flat, but in the opposite direction to make it fluff out. Matted fur will have to be carefully cut out with scissors. If your kitten or cat acts nervously when she hears the clicking of scissors, put adhesive tape on the points of the scissors so as not to injure her if she jerks or jumps when you are clipping her.

One other differing factor in the care of the Persian, compared to that of the domestic cat, is that a valuable cat cannot be allowed to run loose outdoors without being watched. Some Persians will stay in their own back yard if they are trained to do so as kittens. A cat needs some exercise and can be trained to go out for a short time and return on call if rewarded with food each time. One successful cat owner calls her cats home by jingling a spoon against a saucer. Her cats come running when they hear her "dinner-bell."

The Persian will have a thicker coat of fur and better appetite if allowed outdoors. Some cats like to sleep at night in outdoor cages in mild weather. Because of her long fur, a Persian cat is more apt to become sick from hair-balls which she gets in her throat or stomach after cleaning and licking herself. Daily brushing will prevent hair-

This lovely Persian cat is receiving its daily grooming. Routine brushing of this breed's thick, lustrous coat is recommended to prevent matting.

balls to a great extent. A little fish oil from a sardine or tuna can each week will help eliminate hair-balls. Allow your cat to eat grass and feed her a little mineral oil, if she starts to choke on hair-balls in her throat and the fish oil doesn't help.

Your veterinarian can advise you on the necessary distemper, rabies, and cat fever shots, along with eye and ear care, treatment of ringworm, etc. Your pet shop can advise you on the best flea and mite powders, and daily food requirements. Raw eggs, cottage cheese, raw kidney, heart, liver or fish are valuable additions to your cat's weekly menu of canned or dry cat food and milk.

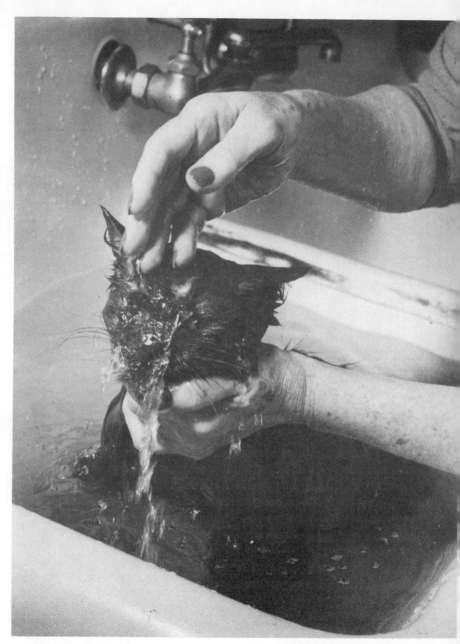

When bathing your cat, you may find wetting the head the most difficult task of all, as it is particularly unpleasant to the cat. Talking to your cat in a gentle, soothing voice will help him to relax.

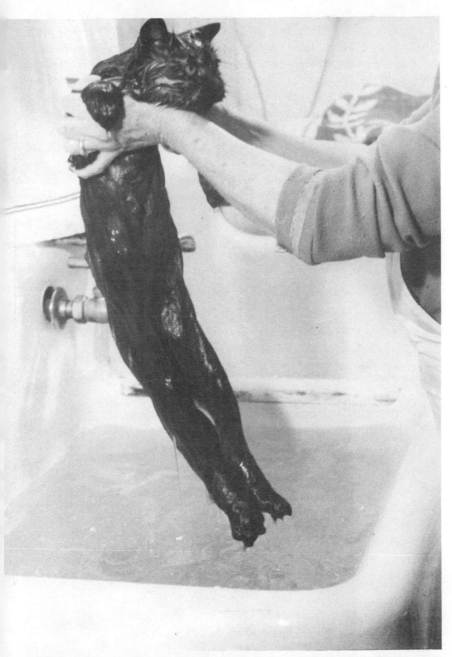

When you have finished washing and rinsing your longhaired cat, be sure to thoroughly dry them down to the skin to avoid the chance of a chill.

Adult Persian female cats usually come in heat in the Spring. This period could last a few weeks if she is not mated. If you want to breed your Persian, select a suitable Persian male. It is wise to have both cats' claws trimmed by a veterinarian before breeding. Leave the male and female Persians together until you are certain that your female is bred. Mark your calendar for 59 to 63 days from this mating; that is when your kittens should arrive. Do not bathe your expectant mother cat, or let her be frightened by dogs or noisy children during her pregnancy. She will have her kittens and care for them with the same ease of the domestic cat.

It is better to breed your Persians and other Deluxe breeds of cats only once a year. Breeding more often is apt to show in the cat's physical condition. Once a year breeding gives your cat a chance to regain her coat and weight between kittens.

A clothes basket is an irresistible temptation for this group of comfort-seeking kittens.

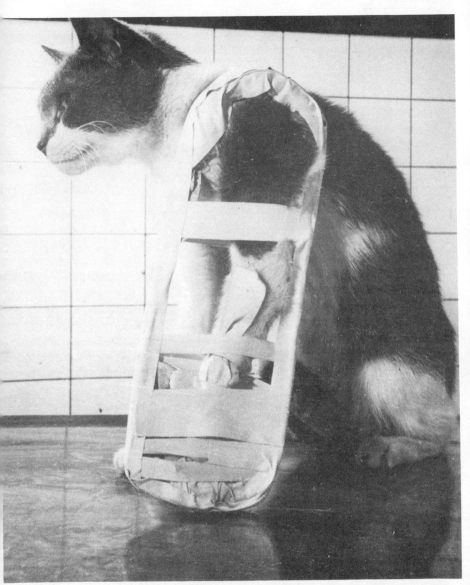

If your cat receives a fracture or major wound, your vet may find it necessary to splint and thoroughly bandage the leg in the above manner. In this way the cat cannot tear at or lick the wound and delay the healing process.

10. Siamese Cats

The Siamese cat was imported into England from Siam (Thailand) in the early 1880's. The Siamese cat was first shown in the United States in 1903 and was immediately popular. A good healthy registered Siamese kitten, with pedigree papers, will cost $25.00 and up.

Siamese cats are active, vital, demanding and very affectionate. They are graceful, fleet, and strong. This breed of cat is particularly popular with men, because of their dog-like characteristics. A Siamese loves to retrieve a thrown ball or toy; it can be taught to lead on a leash and collar, and often loves to ride in the car.

The loud persistent voice of a Siamese cat is annoying to some people. It almost sounds like a child crying. If this voice bothers you perhaps you would be happier with a quieter cat. A Siamese is a real conversationalist, and many cat owners, especially people living alone, enjoy a cat who will "answer and talk".

The Siamese cat has large ears and a long tail. It also has a svelte and a long body. Its eyes should be Oriental shaped, slanting towards its nose and a vivid blue, never green. There are four colors of Siamese cats now recognized in the U.S.A. Listed below is the name and description of each:

1. Seal Pointed: This is the most common type at the present time. The Seal Pointed Siamese has a pale fawn body with deep seal brown points. The mask, ears, legs, feet, and tail are almost black. The nose pad and paws are black.

2. Chocolate Pointed: This Siamese was first recognized in England. They have just recently been shown in the U.S.A. The Chocolate Pointed Siamese has an ivory body with warm, milk chocolate points. The nose pad and paws are chocolate.

3. Blue Pointed: This Siamese has a silvery blue, cold tone body, with greyish darker blue points. The nose, and paws are blue.

4. Frost Pointed: This breed of Siamese has a pale cold body color with bluish grey points that have a definite pinkish cast. They have pink paw pads.

There are other exotic types of Siamese cats not yet recognized or shown. The Red-Pointed Siamese has a white coat with deep red points. The long-haired Siamese is called "Malayan Persian."

The Siamese cat is an exceptionally affectionate breed of a cat, a trait that has led to its abundant popularity.

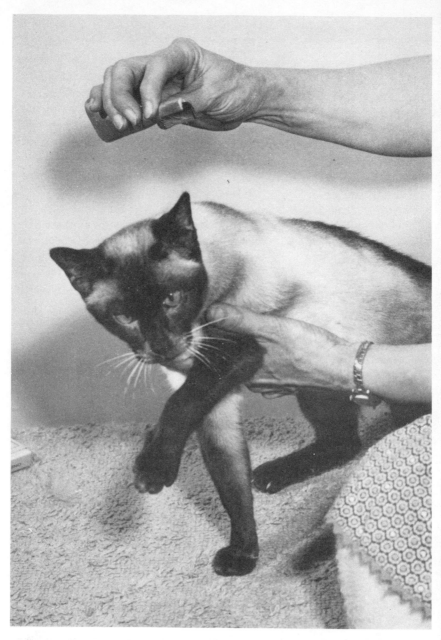

An occasional brushing of your cat's coat will help to remove dead hairs and add sheen. It is advised to start brushing your cat while he is still a kitten so he will learn to enjoy the process, rather than fight against you.

This lucky cat has just been purchased and is one the way to a new home. A portable cat carrier is a convenient way for travelling with your pet.

Because a Siamese has a short smooth coat of fur, this cat is not so apt to swallow hair-balls as the Persian long-haired type of cat. The Siamese sheds heavily in Spring and Summer, and the dead hair should be removed daily to keep the points dark. A brush with a round rubber scalp massager and cat brush are available at your pet shop. Brush the legs and tail too. Do not scratch your cat's skin when combing with a fine tooth flea comb. Shampoos and flea powder with DDT should not be used. Shampoo makes the Siamese cat's fur fluffy and should be used as seldom as possible. It is better to rub corn meal or Fuller's earth into the coat and then brush powder out completely to clean a

Not all cats take kindly to getting a bath—as this Siamese is making abundantly clear.

very soiled Siamese. A few drops of Brilliantine or Lanolin can be used for a dry coat.

If the hair on the cat's ears appears thin, a little bear grease salve or vasoline will encourage hair growth. Gentle rubbing with a soft suede glove, silk material, or even sandpaper gives the Siamese a sleek appearance.

Even though a Siamese cat often likes to take short car rides, a good cat-carrier is advisable for long trips. A carrier will protect a nervous cat from strange sights and sounds while travelling. It is better to line the carrier with paper-towels than with newspapers, as newsprint will sometimes come off on the cat's coat. A small blanket over half of the carrier-bottom will make a cozy bed for your perigrinating feline.

If you wish to breed your Siamese, your pet shop can help you choose a suitable male of the same type. Stud fees will run $10.00 to $100.00. Due to high-breeding, the Siamese are more nervous and high-strung during pregnancy than the domestic cat. It is wise to keep a noisy barking dog far away from the Siamese cat at kittening time. The Siamese female is excitable and might kill her kittens if frightened. A Caesarean delivery is sometimes necessary. The Siamese cannot be bred after a Caesarean and should be spayed. The Siamese kittens are much smaller and more active at birth than domestic kittens. The Siamese kittens are very light at birth and their faces, ears, feet, and tails get sootier as they get older. Their eyes are extremely sensitive to light, and they should be kept in a dimly lit room for the first few weeks after birth. Their eyes should be deep blue.

Ear-mites, worms, enteritis, colds, colic, and skin troubles should be checked and treated by a good veterinarian. NEVER DELAY CALLING YOUR VET WHEN YOUR SIAMESE ACTS SICK. Take its temperature rectally, and if it reads 102° to 104° your cat needs immediate medical care. Cat diseases act so rapidly that a day's delay in taking him to your vet might prove fatal.

The diet of your Siamese will be the same as the Persian and other Deluxe breeds. His food should be room temperature and not cold. He is apt to get colic if he eats ice-cold foods.

A Siamese can wear a collar without ruining his furry coat. Identification tags and rabies tags can be clipped onto his collar. There is a new elastic type collar for sale now which is safer for pets. Pets cannot get caught and strangle on a branch or fence, as they can slip out of the elastic collar if it gets tangled. A little cat-bell will frighten away the birds so that your Siamese can't catch them. Unfortunately the

The muscular hind legs of the Siamese enable them to jump up to six feet with little effort.

You can buy healthy kittens from your pet shop for as little as $5.00, but pedigreed cats will generally cost at least $25.00. The price will vary from breed to breed and depending on the quality of the cat itself, you may have to pay several hundred dollars for a show quality kitten.

bell will also scare the mice and spoil your cat's chances to be a good mouser.

A Siamese cat is another valuable cat that should not have a domestic cat's freedom. His exercise and outings should be carefully supervised, and he should be trained to return on hearing his name.

Madeline Miller, in her T.F.H. booklet "Siamese Cats As Pets" gives a wonderful list of Siamese names and their meanings, if you are looking for a good Siamese name for your new kitten.

A Siamese may be more independent and headstrong than other cats, but he should be disciplined. If he forgets that he is housebroken, he should be penned away from the family for a few hours after each mistake. The Siamese is very intelligent and should learn to use the deodorized grit and outdoors even more quickly than the domestic kittens.

He is apt to be unpredictable, so if he still sharpens his claws on furniture and drapes, after you have patiently shown him the pet shop scratching-post, you may have to spank him with a newspaper or not allow him in the same room with your best furniture. Neutering will *settle* the Siamese male who is strictly a pet and not used for stud.

Your Siamese pet likes his own basket or box-bed. He is a loving pet for children besides being a show-off and an entertainer. The Siamese is a real character who will win the hearts of every member of his family with his silly antics and his overwhelming affection. This is one fellow it won't hurt to spoil with attention and care, for he'll more than pay you back with love.

Teach your children not to tantalize animals that are strange to each other. Not only is this dangerous to the animals involved, but the child might get scratched or bitten in the fury.